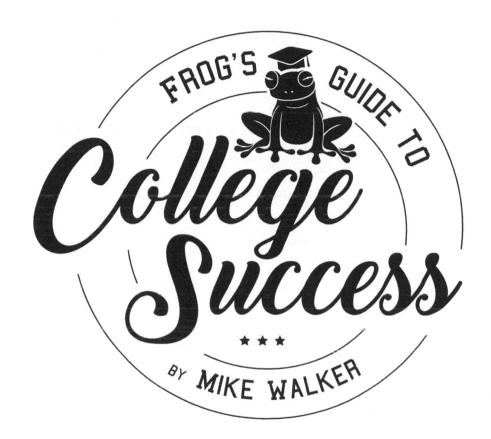

FROG'S GUIDE TO

College Success

★ ★ ★

BY MIKE WALKER

INFINITY
PUBLISHING

ISBN 978-1-4958-2044-1

Printed in the United States of America

Published September 2017

INFINITY PUBLISHING
1094 New DeHaven Street, Suite 100
West Conshohocken, PA 19428-2713
Toll-free (877) BUY BOOK
Local Phone (610) 941-9999
Fax (610) 941-9959
Info@buybooksontheweb.com
www.buybooksontheweb.com

You might be wondering why the book is entitled "Frog's Guide." This photo might help clear this up. When our youngest daughter Kendall was two years old and on the beach in Cape Cod, we took a photo of her and decided she looked like a frog... legs bent, tongue sticking out. From there forward her nickname was Frog. As she was graduating from high school and heading off to college I gave her a first draft of this book intended to help her be successful in college. So I have her to thank for inspiring this project.

Introduction

Life comes at you fast. If you are the parent of a college student like I am, you spend a lot of time asking yourself, "How can I possibly already be old enough to have a kid in college? Just yesterday I was in college myself!" If you are a college student you are asking yourself, "What happened to high school? It was a blur! Am I really ready for college? Will I like it? Can I actually succeed at the college level?"

In many ways I have been in college as long as I can remember. As far back as high school I knew I wanted to go to college. I was the first from my family to ever sit in a college classroom. I was terrified. Then I spent five years earning a bachelor's degree, another two earning a master's degree, and another five earning a doctorate. But trust me...I'm living proof that anyone who works hard can make it in college.

Beyond attending college, I have worked as a college administrator and faculty member for 25 years. So I've seen a thing or two on college campuses. Between attending college, working at colleges, and sending two kids to college, I have a few thoughts on what it takes to get the most of the college experience that might benefit students and families navigating the college phase.

So this is what inspired Frog's Guide. I hope it helps you make college the best four, or five, or six years of your life.

Mark Twain once said, "The two most important days in your life
are the day you are born and the day you find out why."
College helps you discover the WHY.

Respect your *art*.

Whatever you do, attempt to be excellent at it.

No. 2

Ask good questions;
seek good answers.

No. 3

Remember how *big* you can be...

Be extraordinary, universal, transformative.

Don't go among the meek and timid, and don't drown in

the noise and static of life.

No. 4

Envision the life you want and make it *exceptional.*

Remember how small you are...Be humble.

Respect all creatures in this universe.

No. 5

Be *kind* to everyone.

No. 6

Use different *voices* for different situations.

Stand up for yourself and be assertive when necessary.

**Someone is *working harder*
than you and wants it more.**

No. 8

**Someone is working *even harder*
than you and wants it *even more.***

Every day you are the author of the story of your life— *The Great American Novel.*

What peaks and valleys will today's chapter include?

What suspense can you provide your readers?

What magic can you conjure in your story, leaving your readers on the edge of their seats, hurriedly turning the next page?

No. 10

Hold yourself to the *highest standards*, and be your own biggest cheerleader.

Remember to be your own
worst critic.

There is always room for improvement. But don't strive to be totally perfect. Versus being perfect, just be the perfect version of you. Happiness trumps perfection.

No. 12

Close your eyes and *picture the future* **you want.**

Then make a list of how to get from where you are to

where you see yourself in the future. Close the gap.

Don't ever feel *locked in* once you make a decision.

Changing majors, boyfriends and girlfriends, and careers are a part of life. Continually ask yourself, "Am I 100% happy?" If not, reassess.

No. 14

Take it all seriously, but have *fun*.

"The college years" are said to be the best

we will ever have.

No. 15

Take some *risks*...within reason.

No. 16

Take time to practice
being *gracious*.

Surprise someone who influenced your life recently or

years ago with a phone call, or email, or letter, just to

say thank you. It will make their day and it will

help you grow as a person.

No. 17

Write yourself an occasional note to tell you how *great* you are.

You're right where you need to be.

No. 18

Listen as much as you speak, and listen as well as you hear.

Much can be learned when we simply listen.

No. 19

Be present with those around you.

In the presence of others practice being

"present in the moment" with them.

This is how to connect with others.

No. 20

Good *eye contact* and a firm *handshake* will enable others to take you seriously.

High fives, fist bumps and hugs work too.

No. 21

Use all your senses
to *experience* the world.

Open your eyes to the sights around you, smell warm

bread before you taste it, taste everything once, hear

the music of the street, touch things to discover

whether they are coarse or smooth. Make life a

sensory experience.

No. 22

Make time to *see beauty*,
however you perceive it.

Create beauty.

No. 24

Find your *rhythm* and *connect* with life's rhythm.

There is a harmony that exists around us that can be

embraced if we pause to feel it.

Clean **your dorm room.**

Well, at least once in a while.

No. 26

Someone once said that there is no sound more appealing to one's ears than their *own name.*

Get to know other people by name and they

will trust you as a person.

No. 27

The most *thrilling* and most *terrifying* thing for a writer is the blank page.

Put your thoughts on paper, especially

moments that are fascinating.

No. 28

When someone new *introduces* themself to you, if their name is the same as someone you already know, picture the person you already know in your head and focus on this person for 5 seconds.

This will help you remember the new person's name. Waiters and waitresses love it, and you will get better service as a result.

Go *antiquing* with a friend.

One person's junk could be the coolest thing to adorn

your dorm room.

No. 30

Eat *healthy.*

It will give you more energy than sugar and caffeine.

Clean your dorm room *before* your mom visits.

This will balance out for the times she pays you a

surprise visit and it looks "lived in."

No. 32

If you are obsessive about a clean room, leave it *messy* sometimes.

Life is not always in perfect order. Some of the

most brilliant people can't tie their own shoelaces.

Appreciate the beauty of the abstract.

Spend time each day
finding your center.

Listen to your heart beat, feel your chest rise and

fall as you breathe. Block out the noise and connect

with your own rhythm.

No. 34

Better to *get up early* and take an afternoon nap than sleep in (except on weekends).

If you are a caffeine addict, buy your own beans, a cheap electric grinder, and a *French press.*

The coffee will taste better and you will save a fortune versus daily trips to Starbucks.

No. 36

Make a *to-do list* and check things off as you complete them.

College success is about getting organized and approaching every day as though it is a job. Make sure your to-do list includes an hour in the library for every hour in the classroom.

No. 37

Do a few push-ups and sit-ups
every day.

Mini push-ups and sit-ups qualify.

No. 38

Remember looks *aren't* everything.

Be comfortable in your own skin.

No. 39

Complete the things on your to-do list as soon as possible.

This feels much better than procrastinating.

It's the easiest way to feel like we are actually

accomplishing something.

No. 40

Pay others *compliments*, and seek
to be around people who
complement you.

Learn the difference between
homonyms and homophones.

No. 42

Be emotionally *strong*.

Tears are ok as long as you can also stand firm, look

someone in the eye, and say, "I'm sorry, I disagree with

you," or "I'm sorry, but your words are offensive." You

may feel terrified when you say it, but they will never

know it if you don't show it.

No. 43

Call your parents when they
least expect it.

No. 44

Don't *embarrass* easily.

Just laugh at yourself and remember in the big scheme of things life's little embarrassments happen to everyone.

Help those who cannot
help themselves.

Hold doors for people who are physically challenged.

Karma will then open doors for you when

you least expect it.

No. 46

Thank military *veterans* for their service.

They sacrificed a lot for our country,

and appreciate that others notice it.

Proofread everything you
submit in college.

Better yet, exchange papers with a friend and proofread

for each other. It will help you catch your own errors

and will improve your writing skills. Some mispellings

are hard to catch.

No. 48

Dance and sing out loud whenever you can, except in class.

Teachers don't generally like such interruptions (unless you're in a dancing or singing class).

No. 49

Listen to your *intuition*.

If a person seems shady or a situation seems unsafe,

it most likely is. Your instinct has been honed for

thousands of years, so trust it.

No. 50

Make a list of some new things
you want to experience, then go
and do them.

Don't put *new things* off.

You will never have more time than while in college to

check out the world around you.

No. 52

Don't call your parents or text them every day.

Break that habit early on so you can take

charge of your life.

**When you first go away to college
your parents will be** *freaking out.*

They need as much help as you during this transition.

Tell them it's going to be ok.

No. 54

Don't just call your parents when you need _money_.

They may stop answering your calls if you do.

Especially as a freshman, approach schoolwork like a *full time gig*.

Go to class, then go to the library.

Read ahead for each class.

No. 56

Seek out *smart people* who have already chosen your major and *pick their brains* about classes and professors.

They've been there, done that.

No. 57

Be a good steward of your *environment*, and teach others to do the same.

Fill your water bottle and don't buy plastic water

bottles. The Earth is choking on them.

Much of your penchant for *happiness* lies in how you approach life, your *perspective*.

You can either be the type of person who starts sentences with "I have to..." or optimistically approach each task with an attitude of, "I get to..." It's a subtle difference, but most of the things we get to do in life aren't so bad, and others would likely be thrilled to be in our shoes.

No. 59

Don't *cut* corners.

There is no replacement for hard work.

No. 60

Wear *sunscreen*.

No. 61

Get into the habit of *properly* *citing* all your work.

Your school takes this seriously, so you should too.

No. 62

After you graduate from college, hopefully you will *write or draw or create something* that is good enough in someone else's eyes that they end up citing you as its author/creator.

No. 63

For an hour each day, *turn off* your computer and your cell phone and take a walk, grab an ice cream, or read the paper.

No. 64

Studies show up to an hour per day on the Internet makes people *happy*, more than an hour per day makes them *anxious*.

Don't live in the virtual world. Live in the real world where people look each other in the eye and talk.

No. 65

Always answer the phone when mom and dad call.

Assume they may be asking you if you

are short on cash.

No. 66

Hold someone's hand.

No. 67

Spend a little time each day, or week, *reading* the newspaper (paper version or online).

Try to keep up with what is happening in the world,

the U.S., and your region. Be an informed consumer of

information, but cut through the gobbledygook.

No. 68

Use new words you have never heard before, like *gobbledygook.*

In college I told my friends I felt "discombobulated" by

my English professor. They thought I was a genius.

Occasionally *reflect* on the people who made *sacrifices* to get you to where you are.

Some of them are looking down on you right now and

taking great pride in your accomplishments.

The people who helped you get here would do it *all over again* just to see you succeed.

You *worked hard* to get in to college.

You'll need to work just as hard to realize your dreams.

Don't let the run-of-the-mill tedium of the day haze your

goals. There will always be excuses for avoiding the

hard work of getting ahead.

No. 72

Always give and garner *respect*.

No. 73

You will never be terrified of being
unprepared **in class if you**
read ahead.

No. 74

Support your school's
athletic teams, including those
that it seems no one cares about.

Your athletes take pride in representing your school,

so show up sometimes to cheer them on.

Wear *face paint* at least once at an athletic event.

Opportunities to wear face paint will, unfortunately,

be less frequent later in life.

No. 76

Keep to a smart diet but try some *different* foods.

Don't skip *breakfast.*

No. 78

If you choose to drink *alcohol*, start with a full stomach, alternate drinks with water, and remember that as soon as you lose control of your ability to *make good choices*, others will be lurking to make poor ones at your expense.

No. 79

Ask questions in class.

Teachers love that sort of thing.

No. 80

Make sure you can have fun
without **the use of alcohol.**

Otherwise your life will be a series of hangovers,

regrets, and harsh realities.

Dance even if you don't dance well.

In college any appreciable body movement is

typically celebrated.

No. 82

Brush your teeth three times a day, and try to floss at least before bed.

Good oral hygiene will keep your whole body healthy,

and will reduce offending people with your breath.

No. 83

Land a job that includes
dental insurance.

No. 84

There is no such thing as
"European hygiene."

Shower every day and use deodorant.

We're not in Europe.

Read your *syllabus* for every class.

READ YOUR SYLLABUS FOR EVERY CLASS!

The author Rudyard Kipling nailed it when he said, "The *Strength* of the wolf is in the pack, and the *Strength* of the pack is in the wolf."

Use the buddy system, especially if you walk at night or off campus.

No. 87

If you need help, ask for it.

No. 88

If you spot someone who
needs help, *offer it.*

No. 89

If you ask questions in class, make sure you already did the *reading* **for the week.**

If you are asking questions to gain favor but don't know

what you are talking about, it will work against you.

Professors are sort of smart people.

No. 90

Introduce yourself to your teachers during their open office hours, especially in your major.

In college getting to know faculty and staff is cool, not brown-nosing. Remember they are just people like you.

When it comes to *finding your way* on campus, learning "how things get done," and fitting in, grab coffee during your first week on campus with an upper-division (junior or senior) student.

They already figured out the ropes and can help you acclimate to your new home.

No. 92

Don't reinvent the wheel.

It's all been done before.

No. 93

Reinvent the wheel.

No. 94

Don't be finite in the number of *friends* you make in college.

Start building your network now, and never,

ever burn bridges. You never know when you may

need even the most annoying people to

help you at some point.

No. 95

Try to learn your *school songs* including the fight song and alma mater.

It's geeky but cool.

No. 96

Your brain is still like a sponge, so you stand a good chance of *retaining* a lot of *what you learn* in college.

Later in life the brain tends to get a bit squishy.

Make time to *meet* your college president.

Just go introduce yourself to them.

It will make their day.

After your freshman year, *get involved* on campus.

Join a few clubs that align with your interests or major,

or try something totally new.

Join a fraternity or sorority if you want to be a *leader*.

Don't join a fraternity or sorority just because you need friends or drinking buddies.

No. 100

Be *patient* **with your new roommate.**

They're freaking out too.

If you and your roommate are *totally* *incompatible* **after all attempts to get along, change rooms.**

Don't spend a whole year in a room with a

person you can't stand.

Learn to *swim* (literally, but also figuratively).

On clear nights take a minute to look out your window or go for a walk to *check out the stars.*

It will remind you of what an amazing universe we

are part of, and how small you are and how fragile

the gift of life is.

No. 104

Find someone you really like and *star gaze* **with them.**

Some things in life are better when shared.

Take *advantage* of your local resources.

You may not often come back to your college town once you graduate.

No. 106

**"Try everything in life once" is
really only a *theory*.**

There are dead people and people with permanent

physical disabilities because they decided to "just try it"

in college. There is a fine line between having fun

and being stupid.

Pace yourself.

Four years of college passes fast, but it's not a sprint.

No. 108

Don't forget to *practice* **your cursive writing.**

It's a wonderfully unique reflection of who you are as different from anyone else on the planet.

Learn to *communicate* well and *write* well.

Employers love to hire people who can convey meaning with accuracy and art. Also, learn to spell versus relying on spell-check to right well.

No. 110

Someone else wants your *dream job* **more than you.**

Forget about high school at least in terms of all the icky parts you experienced.

College is a blank slate. You get to start over and be whoever you want to be.

Keep a *journal.*

*It will help you express your joys and frustrations, it will
be cathartic when you are totally stressed out, and it
will help you chronicle some really funny stuff to look
back on later. You won't be able to locate your cell
phone pictures in 20 years.*

Be mindful of how you characterize yourself in cyberspace.

Assume everything you put out there may be seen not only by your closest friends, but your parents, grandparents, prospective boyfriends/girlfriends and potential employers. No one will hire you if you look like a total wing nut online.

No. 114

Give free *hugs*.

And when someone you care about least expects it,

give a hearty "airport-arrivals-pickup-lane-run-out-of-

the-car-tackling-an-old-friend-hug."

EAT A LOT OF *pizza.*

No. 116

When speaking with others, ask them more *about them* than you tell about yourself.

It is the greatest sign of self-confidence to cater to learning about someone versus bragging about you. If they are grounded, they will be smart enough to also ask you some stuff too. Conversations aren't competitions.

Find some really stupid *intramural games* to compete in.

This is the closest version of "recess"

you are going to find in college.

No. 118

Avoid being with *controlling* people.

They tend to also want to control you.

Don't overdose on caffeine.

While we're at it, don't overdose on anything.

No. 120

Don't put your cell phone, iPad or computer in *bed* with you at night.

When your body is ready to slumber, shut down the

engines, darken the shades and curl up and sleep well.

Your technology will be its usually bedside

intrusion when you awake.

Get used to *popping up* when your alarm goes off.

Coming in late for a professor's lecture is not the same

as sauntering into homeroom late in high school.

You're purchasing someone's expertise in college, and

a professor's ego could be fragile enough to impact

your grade for late or missed classes.

**If you're five minutes early,
you're *on time*.**

Don't wear *head phones*
on your bike.

No. 124

You really should *wear* a bike *helmet*, even if it's totally uncool.

No. 125

Buy rain *boots*.

Sitting in class with wet feet and socks sucks.

No. 126

Check the *weather* forecast.

Someone gets paid to help you predict whether to wear

a tee shirt or a coat. In the winter, be ok with a scarf,

hat and mittens. There are limited hard fashion

rules in college. About anything goes.

No. 127

Take some fun and weird *electives* like "Museums, wine and zombies."

No. 128

Don't *jog* along the roadway.

This is what you pay a recreation fee for. Someone more distracted than you is driving a car on the same road you run on. Jog on a sidewalk or in your campus rec center.

No. 129

Buy an *umbrella* **and**
a *rain jacket.*

No. 130

If you have to wear *make-up*
to impress someone, re-think
your peer group.

Make sure people dig you for who you are.

No. 131

A great way to *save money* in college is to wear less make-up.

Try a _different_ hair-do.

This will freak out your family and close friends but will

totally liberate you.

Shave your head at least once.

But remember that hair grows back, tattoos are

another story.

No. 134

If weed isn't *legal* in the state where your college is, it really doesn't matter how many other states have *legalized it.*

Don't get *kicked out* of college for violating their rules.

It's not worth it, even though McDonalds

needs plenty of cashiers.

No. 136

Be careful about talking *politics*
and *religion*.

It usually ends badly.

If you talk politics and religion, state your belief and then *let others state theirs.*

There are few absolute truths when it comes to P&R. Beliefs are as subjective as your favorite color. You most likely are not going to convince an opposing adolescent that your beliefs make more sense than theirs.

No. 138

Smoking cigarettes in college is *the worst* time to start.

It will drain your money, damage your health, and may

be a habit that follows you years after. If you haven't

started smoking at 18, just tough it out.

E-cigs are equally *nasty.*

Do we really know what they put in that stuff? Some marketing wiz came up with the word "vaping" just to get you to try it.

No. 140

Study all sides of an issue, especially the *converse side.*

Try to back up your points with facts. You know what they say about opinions.

College is one big *beautiful mess,*
sort of like life.

Check out *live* bands.

If your ears are still ringing a bit in the morning, you probably had a good time. Don't sit too close to the speakers, unless you are trying to avoid that person in the bar who you really don't want to talk to. Then if they approach you, just point to your ears and raise your hands in the air as though you can't hear a word they are saying.

Be *passionate* about things but *compassionate* about others.

You will meet meat-eaters, vegetarians, vegans, atheists, Muslims and anarchists. Like picking a meal off a menu, try to sample the broad range of people you meet in college.

Don't buy *pets* in college.

That stuff is what you will do when your kids go off to college and you get lonely with their absence. For now, you have enough on your hands without rushing out of class to go walk Fido.

Don't take your eyes off any of your
valuables **anywhere on campus.**

No. 146

**If you *like* someone,
keep seeing them.**

If you don't, find a nice way to tell them you aren't

interested. Don't let people you don't like hover about.

Use your words.

I'm too far removed from college to give advice on *dating* versus *hooking up.*

Bottom line is, assume everyone you meet is totally

virtuous or totally infected. Also assume anyone who

wants to have unprotected sex with you already has a

horrible disease that will cause extreme pain to your

most sensitive body parts. Condoms are usually

free in your health center. Use them.

No. 148

Kindergarten teachers already gave you the *perfect plan* for success in college—SHARE, SAY PLEASE AND THANK YOU, TAKE NAPS, HAVE COOKIES FOR SNACK, PAY ATTENTION, and HAVE FUN.

The rest takes care of itself.

If something sounds too good to be true, *it probably is.*

Use your Spider Senses to differentiate a free meal

from a scam. There are no free meals.

Don't get a job your first semester.

Also, don't rush to enroll in graduate school... Be

patient with the job market. It's as fickle as the Chicago

Bears' choice of a starting quarterback.

Start a draft of a *resume* your freshman year.

At least keep a file of the stuff you would put on a resume. Go to your career center no later than your sophomore year and ask them to help you with a resume. That's what you pay a career center fee for. If you wait until the week before graduation to create a resume, it's too late.

No. 152

Beer swilling *frat guys* **are funny, but if you spend too much time with them you will be known as the girl who hangs out with beer swilling frat guys.**

If you hang out with frat guys, *don't pass out* at the frat house.

Just trust me on this one.

No. 154

College offers so much more than
beer swilling frat guys.

$\mathcal{N}$ot all fraternity men are beer swillers.

Test the various stereotypes that emerge from the American college experience.

No. 156

Use *coupons.*

Catch deals offered to college students. They're out there if you look. You can be the big spender after you make your first million.

Name drop a few plays, performers or artists you have experienced.

It will impress people.

No. 158

Money isn't everything.

Plenty of college graduates choose noble professions

in public service and helping others. Decide what you

most enjoy doing, and see if that can be your career.

If you graduate and you don't have a job, _move back in_ with mom and dad, mooch off them, and contemplate your options.

It's a safe play, and they will dig having you back.

No. 160

**Don't live with mom and dad for too
long; that's actually** *not cool.*

When you get to college, *send a note* to your high school teachers that you most liked and who helped you the most.

Consider being a teacher.

It doesn't pay much but it's one of those careers where you can truly make a positive impact on the world. And you will have summers off to do other stuff.

Support the *Arts.*

Life imitates art and art imitates life. So we are really all just actors on one big stage. You will learn a lot about life, human emotion and yourself when you see a play, hear a performance, or view art work.

No. 164

In college *tutoring* is for the kids who want to get ahead, and doesn't carry the same negative stigma it did in high school.

No. 165

When on campus, if you see an employee taking out the trash or sweeping a hallway or fixing a light bulb, stop and *say thank you.*

They contribute toward your school just like your president and professors.

No. 166

Thank *campus police* for their work.

Get to know them. You never know when this may come in handy, and they will appreciate you recognizing their efforts to help keep you safe.

Don't assume a cop will keep you safe.

Make safety your own priority.

Only you can manage you.

No. 168

If your college offers tutoring, *take advantage* of it.

It's usually free, sometimes taught by students who already passed the same classes you are enrolled in, and will help you feel more confident academically.

Wear *funky* pajamas.

Actually do this even after you graduate from college.

Always strive to nurture your inner kid.

College is *Stressful.*

But separate positive stress from negative and find outlets to manage your stress. Negative stress is the death of a close friend, being robbed off campus, or being kicked out of college. Positive stress is the pressure you will feel to manage your time and pass your classes. Good news is there are tons of people on your campus paid to help you with your stress.

"*Study aids*" like Adderall and other drugs aren't really necessary for you to focus unless your doctor tells you so.

Generally focus comes from practicing on how to hunker down and connect your eyes to your brain.

No. 172

No-Doze is legal but is essentially the same as lots of *caffeine.*

Just pick a study strategy that works for you and stick

to it. Generally, over-prepare for your exams.

It's *not uncool* to keep a photo of your parents in your dorm room.

This will make your mom cry as she drops you off for college, which is standard.

Select a few personal items from your bedroom to *bring along* to school.

But leave your HS letterman jacket (shoot, they haven't worn those since the 70's, sorry) behind. Everyone was a star in HS. Pick a few favorite things that will inspire you or help you relax. A favorite blanket, pillow, or teddy bear is not an uncommon feature in college dorm rooms.

**Remember if you are in college, in
some way or another you are among**
the privileged few **in the world
who have access to learning from the
brightest minds on the planet.**

Don't take this opportunity for granted.

Live on campus for your first two years, then move off campus (but where the crime rate is low and tenants can actually get some sleep).

If you pick a place that is party central, anticipate a correlation between the amount of sleep you will get and your GPA.

Keep doing *community service.*

The world needs your help.

You *don't* really need a car in college your first year.

If you bring one, start it every two weeks so the battery

doesn't die, charge other students gas money if they

ask you to chauffeur them to the grocery store or

Walmart, and don't forget to get your oil changed every

3,000 miles. Mom and dad won't do that

for you anymore.

Don't serve as the *designated sober driver* for your drunk roommates.

Helping people is noble, but enabling your roommates isn't. Let them take a taxi or Uber if they want to overconsume. Scraping dry vomit off your floor mats isn't something you can put on your college transcript.

No. 180

If you choose to overconsume,
make sure you have some sober
friends around, and always take a
safe ride home.

But don't overuse this privilege.

No. 181

Your *reputation* **is everything.**

No. 182

Don't change your religious, non-religious, or spiritual beliefs just because you are in college, unless it occurs to you that you were only adopting your parents' beliefs all along.

You're an adult now, so you get to make all the big decisions from here forward.

Many *happy people* are successful, but not all successful people are happy.

As you decide what college will offer your future, make sure you are not sacrificing happiness for material wealth. No amount of money can make you happy.

No. 184

Go somewhere *fun* for spring break
at least once while in college.

Study abroad, but pick a place
that is safe and where you won't
be exploited.

No. 186

Learn a *second language* while
in college.

Call your brother or sister when they least expect it.

Your family will be your steady rock for the rest of your life. Don't let your ties to your siblings languish while you're away at school.

No. 188

Sit down with an elderly person and *inquire* about their life.

Their story will fascinate you.

Lock your room.

Your dorm may seem like one big pajama party, but as soon as you trust that all your stuff is secure, your laptop will disappear. College is no more or less safe than where you grew up.

No. 190

Be *curious* about stuff you know nothing about.

College is the time to know north from south, how the earth's rotation impacts seasons and why the belief that bears hibernate in the winter is a myth. Learn as much as you can.

If you don't like *cold weather,* don't pick a school where it snows.

If you pick a school where it snows, spend a few

weekends on the slopes.

No. 192

When you look in the mirror, don't forget to *look* yourself in the eye.

Looking good is important; being good is

more important.

Practice having *integrity*, which means doing the right thing even when no one is watching.

No. 194

Always tell the truth.

Covering lies is hard work and always fails.

If you take a *road trip* to visit a friend at another college, do your homework before you go.

You won't get any done once you arrive,

trust me.

Do a word count of this book
for the word *"self."*

It appears in various forms 17 times. The word "other"

appears 21 times. Endeavor to be "other-centered."

You spend every minute of your life with yourself. Try

to spend a good chunk of it with and thinking about

others. The person who receives the most thank you

cards in life is declared the winner.

Seek things and people who *open your eyes* and quicken your pulse.

These are your callings and your life partners.

No. 198

**Know when you've *run out*
of things to say.**

If you get to 198 pieces of advice for college students

and you've said everything you wanted to, don't

stretch it to 200 just because it's a nice, even number.

Life has too much order to be constricted by

rules that aren't real.

Always find *one more thing* to say.

Don't go through college without speaking your voice.

You matter. Mostly though, have fun. It will be a

fascinating but fast four years.

Made in the USA
Middletown, DE
13 January 2019